THE LOCH NESS MONSTER

By Marty Erickson

Published by The Child's World®
1980 Lookout Drive • Mankato, MN 56003-1705
800-599-READ • www.childsworld.com

Photographs ©: Shutterstock Images, cover, 1, 2–3, 5, 6, 10–11, 12, 16–17, 19, 21, 23; iStockphoto, 7; Daniel Eskridge/Shutterstock Images, 9; AP Images, 13; Victor Habbick/Shutterstock Images, 15; Rostislav Stefanek/Shutterstock Images, 20; Daniel Eskridge/Shutterstock Images, 24

Copyright © 2022 by The Child's World®
All rights reserved. No part of this book may be reproduced or utilized in any form or by any means without written permission from the publisher.

ISBN 9781503850286 (Reinforced Library Binding)
ISBN 9781503850811 (Portable Document Format)
ISBN 9781503851573 (Online Multi-user eBook)
LCCN 2021939636

Printed in the United States of America

Table of CONTENTS

CHAPTER ONE

FINDING NESSIE

Tourists line the shore of Loch (LOCK) Ness in Scotland. They sit in plastic chairs on the bank and the road that runs alongside the lake. Some tourists even go out into the lake on boats. They are all hoping to catch a glimpse of the famous Loch Ness Monster, or "Nessie."

The lake is calm. A warm summer breeze moves through the grasses. Everyone keeps their eyes on the water. They had all heard the **rumors** of a huge creature lurking in the water. They saw the photos. People wanted to believe the creature was real. If they could catch the Loch Ness Monster on camera, then the whole world would know the truth.

Loch is the Scottish word for "lake." Loch Ness is a large freshwater lake near Inverness, Scotland.

Visitors to Loch Ness can take boat tours to try to spot the Loch Ness Monster.

The tourists fidget in their seats. Hours pass by. A few ducks splash into the lake. Everyone turns to take a photo. Sighs echo through the crowd. There is no sign of Nessie. A long neck does not arch out of the water. Flippers do not splash. There is not even a tiny monster-shaped wave in the distance.

When the sun sets, the tourists pack up their belongings. Nessie had not made an appearance. But it had only been one day. Many of the visitors will not give up so easily. There is still a chance the Loch Ness Monster is out there. It may be just a matter of time before someone captures it on camera.

No photos claiming to show the Loch Ness Monster have captured the creature's full body.

CHAPTER TWO

HISTORY OF THE LOCH NESS MONSTER

Legends of the Loch Ness Monster come from the Scottish Highlands. Loch Ness is a lake. It is about 23 miles (37 km) long and near the town of Inverness. Loch Ness is also deep. The lake is more than 800 feet (240 m) deep in some places.

Stories of the Loch Ness Monster are more than 1,000 years old. A group of people known as the Picts lived in Scotland. They carved images into rocks. Researchers found images of a creature that looked similar to modern descriptions of the Loch Ness Monster.

Throughout history, many people have told stories about Nessie.

Another story of a creature in Loch Ness happened in 565 AD. It said a creature tried to attack a person. Saint Columba sent the creature away.

Some people think swimming circus elephants may be an explanation for the Loch Ness Monster. Circuses were common near Inverness in the 1930s, and they often had elephants.

Modern sightings of Nessie began in 1933. One family claimed they saw a creature cross the road in front of their car. They said it dove into the lake.

A year later, a newspaper published a photo of something that looked like a creature in the water. The article claimed it was proof of the Loch Ness Monster. Around the same time, a hunter found tracks leading from the woods to the lake. Researchers made copies of the tracks.

Both the photo and the tracks were **hoaxes**. The tracks came from a stuffed hippo foot. Sources in the 1990s revealed the photo was fake. The photographer had attached a wooden cutout to a toy submarine.

This famous 1934 image caused many people to believe in the Loch Ness Monster. It was later proven to be a hoax.

Some people say the Loch Ness Monster may be a plesiosaur. Plesiosaurs were a type of marine reptile. They lived at the same time as dinosaurs. Descriptions of the Loch Ness Monster resemble plesiosaur fossils.

Plesiosaurs lived between 80 and 215 million years ago.

But **skeptics** say it is unlikely the Loch Ness Monster is a plesiosaur. The area around Loch Ness froze during the last **Ice Age**. The Loch was formed 10,000 years ago. Plesiosaurs died out long before that. Loch Ness is also too cold for plesiosaurs.

CHAPTER THREE

CREATURE OF THE DEEP

Legends say the Loch Ness Monster is big. It has a long neck and a small head. People believe the Loch Ness Monster is a **predator**. They think it has sharp teeth to catch prey. The Loch Ness Monster would most likely eat fish and other animals in the lake.

Reports have changed over the years. People who say they have seen the creature describe it as being green or gray in color. Early sightings said the Loch Ness Monster had four feet. It could walk on land. Today, most people believe the creature lives only in the lake. It is a strong swimmer. People believe the Loch Ness Monster has four flippers and a tail.

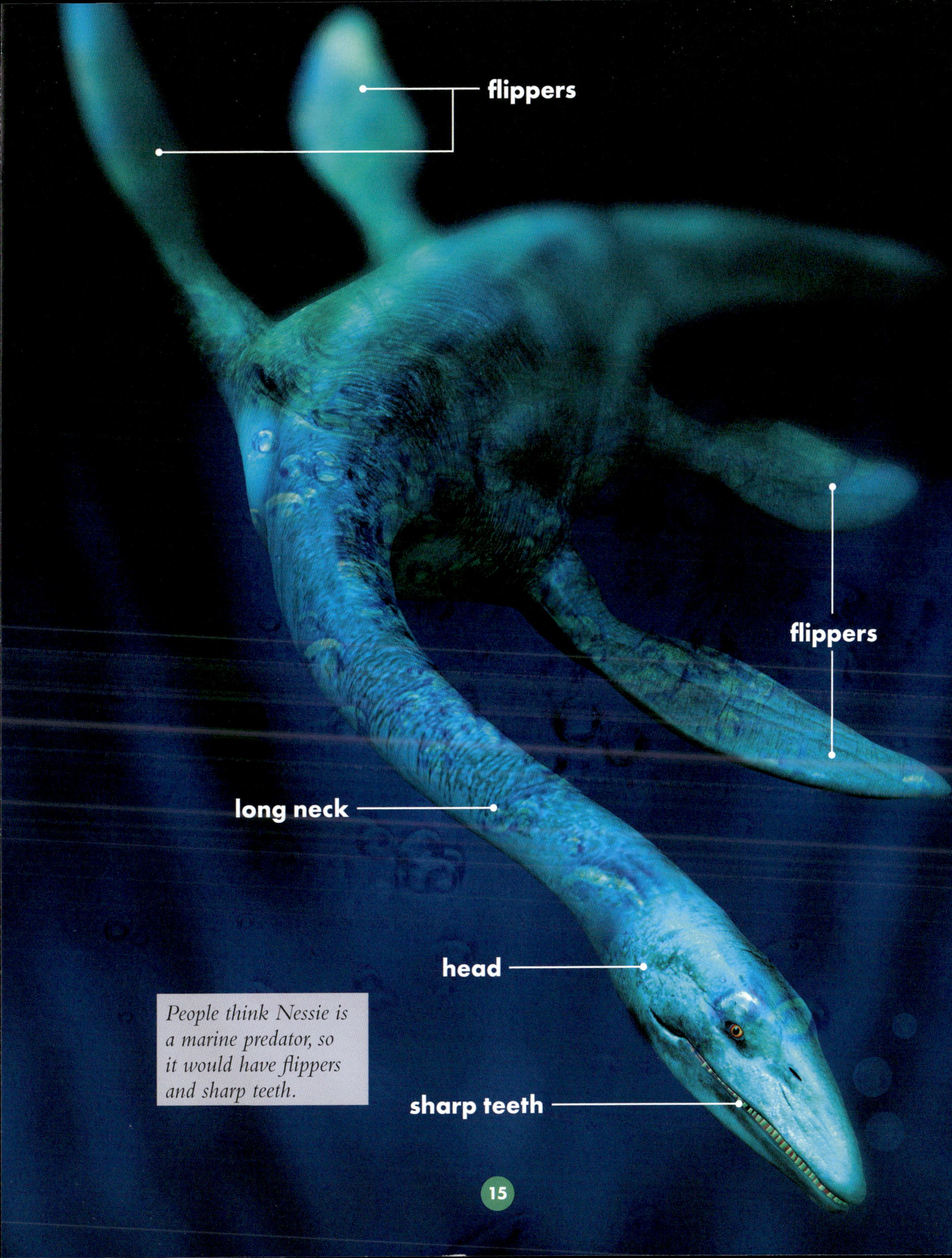

People think Nessie is a marine predator, so it would have flippers and sharp teeth.

People think the Loch Ness Monster is shy. Few people claim to have caught the creature on camera. Even the fake 1934 photo only showed a head and neck. No one has taken a picture of the Loch Ness Monster's whole body.

Sightings continue. Researchers want to learn more about the Loch Ness Monster. If the creature exists, they want to find proof. If it does not exist, researchers want to find an answer to what people are seeing in the lake.

CHAPTER FOUR

THE LOCH NESS MONSTER TODAY

Many researchers study the legends of the Loch Ness Monster. Few photographs show a creature that could be the Loch Ness Monster. Researchers believe people may be seeing a different animal. People might mistake a large animal for Nessie.

Groups of researchers scanned the lake. They used **sonar** to see what was living underwater. Some groups saw images of objects that looked like fins. Some people believed the fins may have belonged to a wels catfish. This type of catfish can grow to be very large. Some are longer than 13 feet (3.9 m).

Native to Asia and eastern Europe, the wels catfish was introduced in Scotland for fishing.

European eels live in Loch Ness. Some researchers say Nessie might be an unusually large eel.

Other researchers believe the Loch Ness Monster could be a giant eel. Scientists took samples from the lake. They found evidence of eels living in the lake. European eels usually grow up to 4 feet (1.2 m) in length. But perhaps Loch Ness is home to one that's even bigger.

The Loch Ness Monster continues to fascinate people. Loch Ness is a major tourist attraction in Scotland. There is a museum in Inverness. It is called Nessieland. The museum educates people about the legends of the Loch Ness Monster. It also talks about the history of the lake and Highlands.

People continue to travel to Loch Ness. People want to see the place where Nessie is said to live. Maybe someday, someone will find proof of the Loch Ness Monster.

The Loch Ness Centre and Exhibition is one of many visitor centers near Loch Ness. Visitors can see this sculpture of the Loch Ness Monster there.

GLOSSARY

hoaxes (HOHK-sez) Hoaxes are events that were faked. The tracks and photograph of the Loch Ness Monster turned out to be hoaxes.

Ice Age (ICE AYJ) The Ice Age was a time in which large portions of Earth were covered in ice. The area around Loch Ness was frozen during the last Ice Age, which ended approximately 11,700 years ago.

predator (PRED-uh-tur) A predator is an animal that eats other animals. Some people think the Loch Ness Monster is a predator.

rumors (ROO-muhrz) Rumors are stories that people tell each other and are usually untrue. After a photo was published, rumors spread about a creature living in Loch Ness.

skeptics (SKEP-tiks) Skeptics are people who doubt whether a claim is true. Skeptics believe the Loch Ness Monster could actually be a large catfish.

sonar (SOH-nar) Sonar uses sound waves to find objects. Researchers used sonar to scan the lake for the Loch Ness Monster.

tourists (TOOR-ists) Tourists are people who travel to visit a place. Tourists come to Loch Ness to try to find the creature living in the lake.

TO LEARN MORE

In the Library

Nagle, Frances. *The Loch Ness Monster.* New York, NY: Gareth Stevens Publishing, 2017.

Oachs, Emily Rose. *The Loch Ness Monster.* Minneapolis, MN: Bellwether, 2019.

Peabody, Erin. *The Loch Ness Monster.* New York, NY: Little Bee Books, 2017.

On the Web

Visit our website for links about the Loch Ness Monster:

childsworld.com/links

Note to Parents, Teachers, and Librarians: We routinely verify our Web links to make sure they are safe and active sites. So encourage your readers to check them out!

INDEX

ABOUT THE AUTHOR

Marty Erickson is a writer living in Minnesota. They write books for young people full time and like to go hiking.